T0380462

MY UNLIMITED JOURNEY

COLOURED REFLECTIONS
- INSPIRING YOU TO BRIGHTEN THE JOURNEY OF YOUR LIFE

Gina Mensah

AuthorHouse™ UK
1663 Liberty Drive
Bloomington, IN 47403 USA
www.authorhouse.co.uk
Phone: 0800 047 8203 (Domestic TFN)
+44 1908 723714 (International)

Because of the dynamic nature of the Internet, any web addresses or links contained in this book may have changed
since publication and may no longer be valid. The views expressed in this work are solely those of the author and do not
necessarily reflect the views of the publisher, and the publisher hereby disclaims any responsibility for them.

Any people depicted in stock imagery provided by Getty Images are models,
and such images are being used for illustrative purposes only.
Certain stock imagery © Getty Images.

This book is printed on acid-free paper.

ISBN: 978-1-7283-9683-5 (sc)
ISBN: 978-1-7283-9651-4 (e)

Print information available on the last page.

Published by AuthorHouse 12/20/2019

authorHOUSE

A little bit about ME - The Author

My name is Eugenia Mensah and I am the Founder of Coloured Reflections, an organisation which inspires individuals to do all it takes to reach their full potential in life, through educational workshops, 1-1/group coaching, networking events and entrepreneurship.

I am a Development Coach and Mindfulness Practitioner who places high value on sincerity and integrity principals. My 'Can Do Spirit' pushes me to always aim to support people in finding creative solutions: 'Inspiring You to Brighten the Journey of Your Life'. I make all efforts to consciously participate in my life, and within the last few years of coaching individuals, I am at a place of confidence in my ability to support people to also participate consciously in their lives and take responsibility!

I have a humble, welcoming and appreciative presence. Firmly I stand for boldness in Truth, Healthy Living and Wealth Creation, embracing and advocating purposeful living through Mental, Emotional, Financial, Social and Psychological stability.

Most of all, I LOVE LIFE and keenly support the development and progress of other people. I have put this planner together as an additional, practical way to support you to WIN!!!!

Users Guide

Your planner has intentionally been designed as an interactive tool to inspire you in becoming an active participant in your life. A way to plan, be mindful and execute goals using a practical resource. The planner encourages you to look at every aspect of your life and will inspire you to pay attention where needed, bettering you to plan efficiently and celebrate growth.

Your planner is filled with 'BIG conversations with self' exercises. These exercises give you a chance to self-reflect. There are many nuggets throughout that will add to your motivation to be the change you would like to see. Written from a high energy field and place of authenticity, I hope you enjoy using your planner as much as I have enjoyed putting it together! I am faithful your planner will encourage you to BE UNLIMITEDLY BOLD and will aid you to 'begin or continue to Walk in Your Purpose with INTEGRITY'.

Get involved in the activities, challenge my views and write down your thoughts. This is private to you, so write what you think and feel. If used correctly, this planner will be with you at all times, along with a pen or pencil.

Acknowledgement

A big thank you to my sister for encouraging and listening to me even in my silence, "if you don't understand my silence, how will you understand my words?" (my favourite quote).

I thank my parents for being so understanding and trying to keep up with my madness in their elderly age!!

I celebrate my friends and family who encourage and support me, in spite of the fact they do not always have a clue what I'm doing day-to-day. Their advice and guidance have been very much appreciated!

Primarily I thank my BOYS: my soldiers, my heartbeats; for being so patient and resilient and keeping me grounded, all LOVE and RESPECT.

The Planner of (FULL NAME)

_____

List all the Weird and Wonderful things about yourself starting with **'I am'**

- I am Thoughtful...

See the Year at a Glance!

2020

January

Su	M	Tu	W	Th	F	Sa
			1	2	3	4
5	6	7	8	9	10	11
12	13	14	15	16	17	18
19	20	21	22	23	24	25
26	27	28	29	30	31	

February

Su	M	Tu	W	Th	F	Sa
						1
2	3	4	5	6	7	8
9	10	11	12	13	14	15
16	17	18	19	20	21	22
23	24	25	26	27	28	29

March

Su	M	Tu	W	Th	F	Sa
1	2	3	4	5	6	7
8	9	10	11	12	13	14
15	16	17	18	19	20	21
22	23	24	25	26	27	28
29	30	31				

April

Su	M	Tu	W	Th	F	Sa
			1	2	3	4
5	6	7	8	9	10	11
12	13	14	15	16	17	18
19	20	21	22	23	24	25
26	27	28	29	30		

May

Su	M	Tu	W	Th	F	Sa
					1	2
3	4	5	6	7	8	9
10	11	12	13	14	15	16
17	18	19	20	21	22	23
24	25	26	27	28	29	30
31						

June

Su	M	Tu	W	Th	F	Sa
	1	2	3	4	5	6
7	8	9	10	11	12	13
14	15	16	17	18	19	20
21	22	23	24	25	26	27
28	29	30				

July

Su	M	Tu	W	Th	F	Sa
			1	2	3	4
5	6	7	8	9	10	11
12	13	14	15	16	17	18
19	20	21	22	23	24	25
26	27	28	29	30	31	

August

Su	M	Tu	W	Th	F	Sa
						1
2	3	4	5	6	7	8
9	10	11	12	13	14	15
16	17	18	19	20	21	22
23	24	25	26	27	28	29
30	31					

September

Su	M	Tu	W	Th	F	Sa
		1	2	3	4	5
6	7	8	9	10	11	12
13	14	15	16	17	18	19
20	21	22	23	24	25	26
27	28	29	30			

October

Su	M	Tu	W	Th	F	Sa
				1	2	3
4	5	6	7	8	9	10
11	12	13	14	15	16	17
18	19	20	21	22	23	24
25	26	27	28	29	30	31

November

Su	M	Tu	W	Th	F	Sa
1	2	3	4	5	6	7
8	9	10	11	12	13	14
15	16	17	18	19	20	21
22	23	24	25	26	27	28
29	30					

December

Su	M	Tu	W	Th	F	Sa
		1	2	3	4	5
6	7	8	9	10	11	12
13	14	15	16	17	18	19
20	21	22	23	24	25	26
27	28	29	30	31		

Yearly Planner

Your Vision

It all starts with a THOUGHT ....
Which becomes a VISION...
and then a GOAL

That's when the work begins: working hard, working smart, thinking outside the box, late nights, early morning, managing negative/positive emotions

A vision board is a practical tool that keeps you focused on specific life goals. It is a firm representation of your desires and aspirations towards feeling fulfilled, and is invaluable for creating clarity and motivation.

Visualisation is one of the most powerful mind exercises you can do. According to the popular book *The Secret*, "The law of attraction is forming your entire life experience and it is doing that through your thoughts. When you are visualizing, you are emitting a powerful frequency out into the Universe." Whether you believe that or not, visualisation works.

With modern lifestyles often being chaotic, it is quite easy to get distracted and feel bombarded in your pursuit for success or happiness, peace, love, etc. The aim of your vision board is to keep you aligned with your personal goals and works best when displayed somewhere conveniently visible. When creating, you can be honest, adventurous and ultimately UNLIMTED!

#Pay ATTENTION to your INTENTIONS   #The Law of Attraction

What is a GOAL? In your own words

SMART GOAL SETTING

- **Specific** – A goal must be clear and not vague or ambiguous.
- **Measurable** – You should be able to assess how far away you are to your goal as you work towards it.
- **Attainable** – Your goal should be challenging but also achievable. It should neither be 'just' a dream and easy enough to not stretch you.
- **Realistic** – The goal should be one that is relevant to your life and circumstances.
- **Timely** – Your goal should have a timescale. For instance, rather than just "I want to learn Spanish", you should say, "I want to be able to hold a good conversation in Spanish by December next year."

Work with 3 to 4 goals at a time, clarifying whether they are short, medium, or long-term goals. Achieving your goals tells a story and informs you of what your next moves needs to be. It is therefore important to challenge yourself, without becoming overwhelmed. You want to enjoy the journey.

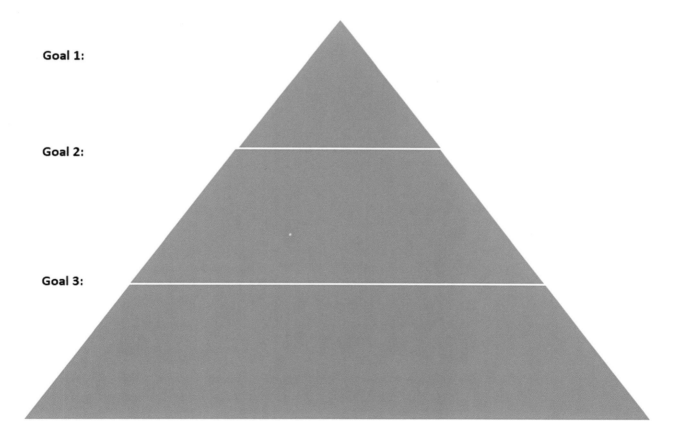

Goal 1:

Goal 2:

Goal 3:

MY GOALS

Why have I chosen these goals?

What is my motivation and driving force behind these goals?

What happens after I achieve these goals?

Who will support me to achieve my goals?

What happens if I don't achieve them?

NOTES: What are your thoughts on this?

(You can add any additional goals here and a step-by-step guide of how you will achieve them). Mind Maps are also a useful and interactive tool to use.

Thought of the Month-January

Manage Your Time – Time Organisation & Management

There is virtue in balancing rest and work – both are necessary and so it is crucial to not overlook either.

Learning to manage your time can present many challenges and conflict. When planning time management, pay attention to what you are using your time for and learn to be selective to maximise productivity. Create the time to reflect, listen to solutions and strategise. By organising your time, you are able to honor your priorities.

Time organisation is not solely about working and following daily routine and schedule. It is essentially about establishing a balance of work, rest and play. When you begin to value your time, you will refuse to waste it. There is a TIME for everything and everything in its TIME.

You can improve your time management and organisation by:

- Use of a diary, planner, notebook or reminders.
- Discipline with your time keeping, to form order and clarity
- Learning the ART of planning ahead, without being too rigid against the natural flow of life.
- Learning to say: 'Not at the moment', 'I will call you back' or I will get back to you', 'It's not convenient right now.'

NOTES: What are your thoughts on this?

December 30, 2019 - January 5, 2020   Week 1

December **30** Monday	
December **31** Tuesday	
January **1** Wednesday	**New Year's Day**
January **2** Thursday	
January **3** Friday	
January **4** Saturday	
January **5** Sunday	

January 6 - 12, 2020   Week 2

January **6** Monday	
January **7** Tuesday	
January **8** Wednesday	
January **9** Thursday	
January **10** Friday	
January 11 Saturday	
January **12** Sunday	

MY GOALS

Why have I chosen these goals?

What is my motivation and driving force behind these goals?

What happens after I achieve these goals?

Who will support me to achieve my goals?

What happens if I don't achieve them?

NOTES: What are your thoughts on this?

(You can add any additional goals here and a step-by-step guide of how you will achieve them). Mind Maps are also a useful and interactive tool to use.

Example of Mind Maps

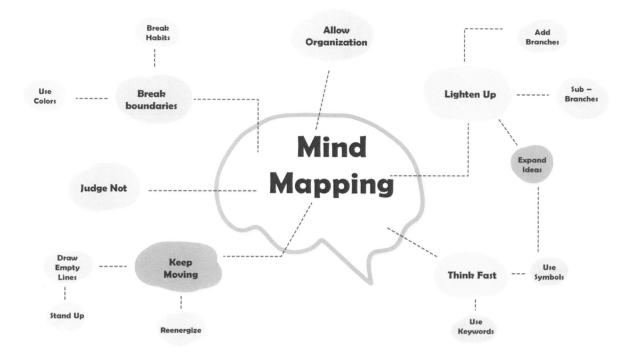

Create your own

January 13 - 19, 2020   Week 3

January **13** Monday	
January **14** Tuesday	
January **15** Wednesday	
January **16** Thursday	
January **17** Friday	
January **18** Saturday	
January **19** Sunday	

Monthly Budget

	Amount			
Income 1				
Income 2				
Income 3				
Expenses	**Amount**	**Budget**	**Actual**	**+/- Difference**
Mortgage/Rent				
Council Tax				
Service Charge				
Electricity				
Gas				
Water				
Internet/Cable				
Mobile Phone				
Food Shopping				
Childcare				
Entertainment				
Loans				
Credit Cards				
Petrol/Travel				
Clothing				
Car Insurance				
Life Insurance				
Health Insurance				
Others				

Monthly Budget

Total Income	Total Outgoings	Remaining	Savings

January 20 - 26, 2020   Week 4

January **20** Monday	
January **21** Tuesday	
January **22** Wednesday	
January **23** Thursday	
January **24** Friday	
January 25 Saturday	
January **26** Sunday	

Financial Matters and Forecast

1. Are you confident in your ability to manage your own personal finances?

2. Do you feel in control of your personal finances?

3. Are your finances a significant worry for you?

4. Do you use a budget planner?

5. Have you set your financial goals for this year?

6. Have you got an action plan in place, as to how you will achieve your financial goals?

7. Are your current income streams able to support your financial goals?

8. If you were unable to work, have you got emergency funds to sustain you for up to 3-6 months?

9. What matters regarding personal finance, would you like a better understanding of?

Mortgages	**Loans**	**Wills Bonds/Stocks/ Mutual Funds**
Insurances	**Debt/Credit**	
Savings	**Investments**	**Pensions & Retirement Plans**

Whichever answers you choose, they are personal to **you**. Research and seek financial advice if needs be!

January 27 - February 2, 2020   Week 5

January
27
Monday

January
28
Tuesday

January
29
Wednesday

January
30
Thursday

January
31
Friday

February
1
Saturday

February
2
Sunday

Thought of the Month-February

Thought Process & Patterns

Our THOUGHTS shape our future. To control their effect, take time to understand your thought processes and patterns, noticing where they have stemmed from and whether your thoughts have embedded during childhood or through personal experiences. Allow yourself to gain clarity of your thoughts, because clarity is a power which produces positive emotions and a sense of order internally.

Every single day, billions of thoughts pop up in our minds. Although these thoughts can be extremely difficult to control, the beauty is, we have the capability to decide and choose the thoughts we FOCUS and give energy to! Thought patterns can change with the right brain training. Not only can you master your thoughts, you can shift your mindset to concentrate on thoughts that elevate and form headspace, to produce more progressive and productive thinking.

What kind of thoughts will enhance your journey and free your mind?

- Do not be afraid to explore and seek professional support to deal with any past negative conceptions and attitudes.
- Use daily positive affirmations and new thought patterns affirmations.
- Challenge negative thoughts – where the focus goes, the energy will flow.

NOTES: What are your thoughts?

February 3 - 9, 2020   Week 6

February **3** Monday	
February **4** Tuesday	
February **5** Wednesday	
February **6** Thursday	
February **7** Friday	
February 8 Saturday	
February **9** Sunday	

February 10 - 16, 2020   Week 7

February
10
Monday

February
11
Tuesday

February
12
Wednesday

February
13
Thursday

February
14
Friday

February
15
Saturday

February
16
Sunday

Self-Reflection Questionnaire

1. What areas in my life need my focus and attention? What kind of focus and attention do they require?

2. Am I open and receptive to new ideas?

3. Am I taking responsibility for my emotions?

4. What am I making excuses to not do?

5. Have I taken responsibility for the condition of my life?

6. Does being alone scare me?

7. What do I want from life?

8. What do I spend the most time worrying about or overthinking?

9. Am I clear on where I am going in my future?

10. Do I put off until tomorrow what could have been done today?

The aim of the self-reflection questionnaire is to start a conversation with yourself to gain a better understanding of where you are. It is beneficial in recognising your characteristics, traits and possible habits that do not serve your productivity. Furthermore, the questionnaire supports the things you are doing well and would like to both maintain and enhance.

There are no wrong or right answers! Self-reflection is not about criticism; it is about knowing which areas in your life can be better supported. Regular self-reflection inspires development and growth. As this questionnaire is not exhaustive, you may want to include further questions that enable you to reflect honestly and regularly.

February 17 - 23, 2020   Week 8

February **17** Monday	
February **18** Tuesday	
February **19** Wednesday	
February **20** Thursday	
February **21** Friday	
February **22** Saturday	
February **23** Sunday	

February 24 - March 1, 2020   Week 9

February **24** Monday	
February **25** Tuesday	
February **26** Wednesday	
February **27** Thursday	
February **28** Friday	
February 29 Saturday	
March **1** Sunday	

Thought of the Month-March

<u>Self-Reflection</u>

Reflecting on yourself honestly is a process involving a willingness to openly explore and analyse the core relationship you have with your character, values and behaviours. Self-Reflection requires a delicate balancing act: paying enough attention to your emotions, without allowing them to affect day-to-day decisions and your ability to meet intentions and priorities.

Do your actions and decisions contain a healthy balance of heart, head and gut instinct? When you ask yourself these important questions, you gain a stronger understanding of your strengths, areas for development, driving factors and direction. This self-task assesses your responses to various situations, while also strengthening your emotional intelligence.

Taking a moment to self-reflect encourages you to look inwards and become clear on your core values. Being fully aware of them, helps to build up your integrity which will in turn lead you to make better decisions and life choices with greater confidence. Regular self-reflection additionally generates opportunity to know exactly where you are at with your time, energy, space and circumstances. This will help you to plan your next moves towards growth and eventually fulfilment.

Self-Reflection Starters

- Use self-reflection and self-evaluation questionnaires as a starting point.
- Be honest, but not critical about your areas for development.
- Create quiet time, reflect consciously in a space where you are safe to explore yourself without rushing or feeling anxious.
- Write down your thoughts and observations. Honest self-reflection must make you feel positively aligned, meaning you are heading in the right direction – keep going! Or uncomfortably unaligned, calling for movement, shifts or changes.

NOTES: What are your thoughts?

March 2 - 8, 2020   Week 10

March 2 Monday	
March 3 Tuesday	
March 4 Wednesday	
March 5 Thursday	
March 6 Friday	
March 7 Saturday	
March 8 Sunday	

March 9 - 15, 2020   Week 11

March **9** Monday	
March **10** Tuesday	
March **11** Wednesday	
March **12** Thursday	
March **13** Friday	
March **14** Saturday	
March **15** Sunday	

How are you doing with achieving your goal – let's Review!

What is your Goal?	What actions are you taking to meet this goal?	What is going well?	What needs re-routing?
To study a masters	I researched the course of my interest, best location and planned a routine which will allow me to study without heavily affecting my work/life balance.	I am enjoying the course, it is really beneficial and I know it will support me in progressing within my career path.	The course workload is heavy and I may need to restructure my daily routine or reduce my working hours.

March 16 - 22, 2020   Week 12

March
16
Monday

March
17
Tuesday

March
18
Wednesday

March
19
Thursday

March
20
Friday

March
21
Saturday

March
22
Sunday

Suggested Reading List

One Soul, One Love, One Heart: The Sacred Path to Healing All Relationships, John E. Welshons (2009)

The 7 Habits of Highly Effective People: Powerful Lessons in Personal Change, Stephen R. Covey (1999)

Redemption, Stanley Tookie Williams, Milo (2004)

Awaken the Giant Within: How to take control of your mental, emotional, physical and financial destiny, Anthony Robbins (2001),

Now Discover Your Strengths: How to Develop Your Talents & Those of the People You Manage, Marcus Buckingham (2005)

The Purpose Driven Life: What on earth am I here for? Rick Warren (2002)

Black Hole Focus: How Intelligent People Can Create a Powerful Purpose for Their Lives, Isaiah Hankel, Capstone (2014)

Emotional Intelligence: Why it Matters More Than IQ, Daniel Goleman (1996), Bloomsbury

The Power of Now: To make **the** journey into **the Now** we will need to leave our analytical mind and its false created self, **the** ego, behind. Eckhart Tolle (2016)

The Enlightened Gardener: Beset by daily life's trials and tribulations, many people search for the elusive wisdom that will help them make sense of their journey and find inner peace. Sydney Banks (2016)

On Becoming a Person: Helping people to discover the path to personal growth through an understanding of their own limitations and potential. Carl Rogers (2004)

5 Love Languages: As practical as it is insightful. Updated to reflect the complexities of relationships today, this new edition reveals intrinsic truths and applies relevant, actionable wisdom in ways that work. Gary Chapman (2015)

Add your own favourite books and books that you would like to read this year!

March 23 - 29, 2020   Week 13

March **23** Monday	
March **24** Tuesday	
March **25** Wednesday	
March **26** Thursday	
March **27** Friday	
March 28 Saturday	
March **29** Sunday	

March 30 - April 5, 2020   Week 14

March **30** Monday	
March **31** Tuesday	
April **1** Wednesday	
April **2** Thursday	
April **3** Friday	
April **4** Saturday	
April **5** Sunday	

Thought of the Month-April

Accepting Personal Responsibility

We are responsible for ourselves and empowerment happens when we take responsibility, ownership and personal acceptance of our lives. Growth also begins the moment you accept responsibility.

Accepting responsibility is not just about behaviour, words and actions. When you take responsibility to lead by example, you enhance the quality of your relationships, as well the management of your internal systems, expectations, personal development and self-improvement. These are all elements of personal responsibility.

It is easy to find fault and lay blame on other people, society and shift responsibility to external factors. While other people and life circumstances can majorly impact our lives, it is ultimately our obligation to choose how we respond and navigate around difficult situations.

Accepting responsibility raises motivation and confidence levels. We are responsible for our thoughts – our actions are a reflection of our thoughts, so it is vital we tune in to them.

NOTES: What are your thoughts?

April 6 - 12, 2020   Week 15

April **6** Monday	
April **7** Tuesday	
April **8** Wednesday	
April **9** Thursday	
April **10** Friday	Good Friday
April **11** Saturday	
April **12** Sunday	

April 13 - 19, 2020   Week 16

April **13** **Monday**	**Easter Monday**
April **14** Tuesday	
April **15** Wednesday	
April **16** Thursday	
April **17** Friday	
April **18** **Saturday**	
April **19** **Sunday**	

Events/Concerts and Fun Time

ACTIVITY	BY WHEN

April 20 - 26, 2020   Week 17

April
20
Monday

April
21
Tuesday

April
22
Wednesday

April
23
Thursday

April
24
Friday

April
25
Saturday

April
26
Sunday

April 27 - May 3, 2020   Week 18

April **27** Monday	
April **28** Tuesday	
April **29** Wednesday	
April **30** Thursday	
May **1** Friday	
May **2** Saturday	
May **3** Sunday	

Thought of the Month-May

<u>Make Your Life Count</u>

As we all know, death in inevitable, so ask yourself these questions:

What legacy would you like to leave behind?

What would you like to be remembered for?

What was your character, behaviour, traits?

What difference did you make to your life and the life of others?

Did you find out who you were on purpose?

Did you answer to your calling and boldly work & walk in your purpose?

Through living in your purpose, your life becomes meaningful, significant, fulfilling, memorable, exciting, effective and productive…. And much, much more! Do not exist, LIVE!!

A few practical ways to make your life count:

- Pay attention to yourself. Which areas need attention and what type of attention?
- Organise and manage your time.
- Study your thought processes and patterns, get to know yourself.
- Self-Reflect honestly and often.

NOTES: What are your thoughts?

May 4 - 10, 2020 Week 19

May **4** Monday	
May **5** Tuesday	
May **6** Wednesday	
May **7** Thursday	
May **8** Friday	**Early May Bank Holiday (75th anniversary of VE Day)**
May **9** Saturday	
May **10** Sunday	

May 11 - 17, 2020   Week 20

May **11** Monday	
May **12** Tuesday	
May **13** Wednesday	
May **14** Thursday	
May **15** Friday	
May **16** Saturday	
May **17** Sunday	

Skills Check & Life Hygiene

What new skills & things have I learnt	How will they benefit and add productivity to my life

May 18 - 24, 2020   Week 21

May **18** Monday	
May **19** Tuesday	
May **20** Wednesday	
May **21** Thursday	
May **22** Friday	
May **23** Saturday	
May **24** Sunday	

May 25 - 31, 2020   Week 22

May **25** Monday	Spring Bank Holiday
May **26** Tuesday	
May **27** Wednesday	
May **28** Thursday	
May **29** Friday	
May **30** Saturday	
May **31** Sunday	

Thought of the Month-June

<u>Who Is In Your Circle</u>

Building and maintaining relationships is one of the most challenging areas for humans. There are 5 regions of our being: Spiritual, Social, Physical, Psychological and Financial. Firstly, ask yourself, who in my circle enhances and supports these regions?

Typically, we focus on relationships with family, friends, work colleagues and business associates, in order to make us feel whole. In particular, you want to pay close attention to people who clap and cheer when you win. Cherish and celebrate the people who demonstrate they have your best interests. And remember, it is not about quantity, but rather *quality*.

Do not be afraid to distance yourself from people who hinder your personal growth, as not everyone wants to support our highest good. People enter in and out of our lives for a reason, perhaps a purpose or a lesson. So do not expect anyone to stay 'forever' irrespective of who they are. Take notice of traffic light signals, in order to build your circle genuinely. It is far more fulfilling to have genuine relationships for a short period of time, than fake relationships over a long period of time!

Do not be sceptical, but be unlimitedly selective when choosing who you allow in your inner circle. This takes strength & wisdom.

- Who supports your goals and motivates you?
- Who allows you to support their goals and growth?
- Who drains your energy and discourages?
- Who do you have truthful/ superficial conversations with?

Remember, everyone is on their own journey and running their own race!

NOTES: What are your thoughts?

June 1 - 7, 2020   Week 23

June **1** Monday	
June **2** Tuesday	
June **3** Wednesday	
June **4** Thursday	
June **5** Friday	
June **6** Saturday	
June **7** Sunday	

June 8 - 14, 2020   Week 24

June **8** Monday	
June **9** Tuesday	
June **10** Wednesday	
June **11** Thursday	
June **12** Friday	
June **13** Saturday	
June **14** Sunday	

June 15 - 21, 2020   Week 25

June **15** Monday	
June **16** Tuesday	
June **17** Wednesday	
June **18** Thursday	
June **19** Friday	
June **20** Saturday	
June **21** Sunday	

June 22 - 28, 2020   Week 26

June **22** Monday	
June **23** Tuesday	
June **24** Wednesday	
June **25** Thursday	
June **26** Friday	
June **27** Saturday	
June **28** Sunday	

Thought of the Month-July

Discover & Create Your Own Uniqueness

Life is about branding ourselves through our identities, discovering our own creativity, potential and talents. Though building our personal brands comes with challenges, fears, excitement and a range of other emotions, the beauty is, we are designed in our own unique way – we should embrace that!

Plant your seeds and position yourself to give, receive and take direction. This leads to your highest good and unique purpose. Use your authenticity and uniqueness to establish strong, personal foundations and practice both strength and conviction in your morals and principals.

Comparing and imitating others often causes disappointment, loss of identity, unhappiness and personal failure.

Life is forever evolving and with that designs a need for continuous discovery. As a strategy may work one day and not another, be unlimited in discovering and creating your own individuality. Enjoy the journey!

- What have you discovered about yourself in the last 3 months?
- What is unique about you?
- What do you love about you?
- Which areas of your life would you like to improve or work on?

NOTES: What are your thoughts?

June 29 - July 5, 2020   Week 27

June **29** Monday	
June **30** Tuesday	
July **1** Wednesday	
July **2** Thursday	
July **3** Friday	
July **4** Saturday	
July **5** Sunday	

July 6 - 12, 2020   Week 28

July **6** Monday	
July **7** Tuesday	
July **8** Wednesday	
July **9** Thursday	
July **10** Friday	
July **11** Saturday	
July **12** Sunday	

July 13 - 19, 2020   Week 29

July
13
Monday

July
14
Tuesday

July
15
Wednesday

July
16
Thursday

July
17
Friday

July
18
Saturday

July
19
Sunday

Mindfulness

```
E K G G C Z J Y E N Y A N F P P G I J S U N I N
D L E D X X Y D G T W Y Q S O F K Q M E H O M U
L Y V P K E U N E A P P N B C T Q U I L O I A X
L D O L X T I F R Z E I J R L A U P N F P T G C
A A T X I H A E T S R N N D A A F W D L E A E N
K T Z T T S N G Q W S R E O R E E C F O F X R W
Y J A A E E M L A C P T X J I C S L U V U A Y F
G R E V S C M X L R E X W L T T A R L E L L W L
G R F S N K N U W R C U E B Y T A K F J N E I E
B H C E O O F A M Q T R G S N R H V N T E R H X
K S U H N Y I I T S I G Q E E V H E R Y S F Q I
E Q F L O L N T J P V L M S P K T F G E S E D B
H H T J I A S T A L E G T M Z S W R E P S M G I
T W J H T H L T D I D C S M I S E P A W X B I L
N D S I A T X T H U C P C L X N I T U B Z R O I
E Q O A R N D M J G R E I A E K I S K O U A E T
C N I N I E K N B E U X R F E E L I N G O T X Y
I G J U P T O F S N O O S P N U U T I D A R H Y
T X O C S N H E U T P A H C P J J L B J A H Q C
C F J E N P N G G L H O E T A A Q U I E T F R A
A T D N I T S B I A T T E N T I V E H I P Q Z V
R H L Z F W F E G S T P E R S E R V E R A N C E
P V J I Y F O C U S N S E R E N I T Y H B O O U
N O I T A Z I L A U S I V S N O I T A T I D E M
```

acceptance	appreciation	attentive	awareness
breathing	calm	clarity	determination
energy	feeling	flexibility	focus
gratitude	hear	hopefulness	imagery
insight	inspiration	joyful	listen
meditation	mindful	nonjudgmental	observation
patience	perserverance	perspective	practice
present	quiet	relaxation	relief
rest	safety	self love	serenity
thankful	thoughts	visualization	

July 20 - 26, 2020   Week 30

July **20** Monday	
July **21** Tuesday	
July **22** Wednesday	
July **23** Thursday	
July **24** Friday	
July **25** Saturday	
July **26** Sunday	

July 27 - August 2, 2020   Week 31

July **27** Monday	
July **28** Tuesday	
July **29** Wednesday	
July **30** Thursday	
July **31** Friday	
August **1** **Saturday**	
August **2** **Sunday**	

Thought of the Month-August

Choose to Keep Moving Forward

No matter what happens in life, regardless of current circumstances, the sun will always rise and set and the clock will always continue to tick.

Avoid letting past experiences dictate your NOW! Find practical ways to process your past and any trauma because you cannot see what is in front of you, if you keep glancing back. Choose to keep moving forwards and break down barriers which block and interfere with your growth and success. There are life lessons in every situation and life is full of variety and choices. Make it your business to arm yourself with countless options so you are left with NO choice but to keep looking ahead.

Challenges come and go, so take a step at a time, day-by-day, be kind and give yourself permission to keep moving forward.

- Is there anything that is blocking you from moving forward with your life?
- If so, what are you going to do about it, what kind of support will you seek?
- What are your good habits and practices that keep you moving forward?
- What motivates you to keep moving forward?

NOTES: What are your thoughts?

August 3 - 9, 2020   Week 32

August **3** Monday	
August **4** Tuesday	
August **5** Wednesday	
August **6** Thursday	
August **7** Friday	
August 8 Saturday	
August **9** Sunday	

August 10 - 16, 2020   Week 33

August
10
Monday

August
11
Tuesday

August
12
Wednesday

August
13
Thursday

August
14
Friday

August
15
Saturday

August
16
Sunday

An Honest Self Evaluation of your Relationships

1. Are you a grateful person? Do you take time to appreciate people you have in your life?

2. Are you focused and attentive when you are conversing with other people?

3. Do you allow time each day to invest in your most important relationships? For example, spending quality time together or doing something meaningful to show loved-ones you care?

4. Do you deal with issues when they come up in your relationships or do you try to avoid those difficult conversations and brush things under the carpet in some way?

5. Do you tend to hold grudges when someone does something you disapprove of, or are you quite a forgiving person?

6. Are you curious about other people, do you take a genuine interest in others and ask questions to better understand them?

7. Are you compassionate towards other people? If someone makes a mistake, would you most-likely be understanding or criticise them for 'getting it wrong?

8. Do you find yourself judging and criticising other people in relation to how well they're performing?

9. What effect do I have on those around me?

10. What expectations am I placing on other people and things?

August 17 - 23, 2020   Week 34

August **17** Monday	
August **18** Tuesday	
August **19** Wednesday	
August **20** Thursday	
August **21** Friday	
August **22** Saturday	
August **23** Sunday	

August 24 - 30, 2020   Week 35

August **24** Monday	
August **25** Tuesday	
August **26** Wednesday	
August **27** Thursday	
August **28** Friday	
August **29** **Saturday**	
August **30** Sunday	

Thought of the Month-September

Nothing Changes Until You Do

There are many interesting views as to whether people can or cannot be changed. I believe if you want to sincerely change, you can! Change does not mean transforming to a new person free from flaws; change is about growth and accepting the natural process and progression of life. Change is the one constant thing guaranteed in the world.

If you are in a place where you truly want things in your life to change, you must firstly begin to change past habits that do not align with your new direction. Certain habits may have worked for you previously, but when the music changes, so must the dance! We have to adapt our habits, ways of thinking, actions and sometimes belief systems accordingly. Change is about being wise and flexible, using past and current experiences to inform us when adjustment is needed and desired.

When contemplating change, always begin by asking why – what is the purpose? Change is extremely personal and must be treated with respect and allowance of appropriate time.

- At this current moment, what things do I need to change?
- Are these changes to benefit me and my purpose, or is it for others?
- What practical things will I do to make these changes?

NOTES: What are your thoughts?

August 31 - September 6, 2020   Week 36

August **31** Monday	August Bank Holiday
September **1** Tuesday	
September **2** Wednesday	
September **3** Thursday	
September **4** Friday	
September 5 **Saturday**	
September **6** Sunday	

September 7 - 13, 2020   Week 37

September
7
Monday

September
8
Tuesday

September
9
Wednesday

September
10
Thursday

September
11
Friday

September
12
Saturday

September
13
Sunday

September 14 - 20, 2020   Week 38

September **14** Monday	
September **15** Tuesday	
September **16** Wednesday	
September **17** Thursday	
September **18** Friday	
September **19** **Saturday**	
September **20** Sunday	

September 21 - 27, 2020   Week 39

September **21** Monday	
September **22** Tuesday	
September **23** Wednesday	
September **24** Thursday	
September **25** Friday	
September **26** Saturday	
September **27** Sunday	

Thought of the Month-October

Manage Your Mind

Our minds are arguably one of our greatest and most powerful assets. But they are easily neglected due to the constant fast-paced lives we live. The demands of conflicting priorities can often make us operate in auto-pilot mode, stopping us from managing our thought processes. An unhealthy mind may lead to a range of long-lasting problems in all areas of our lives. Your mental state is the backbone of who you are and needs to function stably and rationally.

Our minds can have a way of playing tricks on us, but you can play an active part of that game! Take control by not allowing internal battles, insecurities and other negative emotions win.

Apart from your mind, you also have your heart and gut; learn to use all THREE to make solid decisions and choices.

A few Tips for a Healthy Mind:

- Take time out to speak to your mind, nurture your mind, and allow your mind to be your friend.
- Reflect and declutter every day, even if it is for a few minutes.
- Rest and listen often to what your mind is telling you, that way, you can manage intrusive and unwanted thoughts better.
- Your mind believes what you tell it, feed it with love, encouragement, positivity and clarity.

NOTES: What are your thoughts?

September 21 - 27, 2020   Week 39

September
28
Monday

September
29
Tuesday

September
30
Wednesday

October
1
Thursday

October
2
Friday

October
3
Saturday

October
4
Sunday

October 5 - 11, 2020   Week 41

October **5** Monday	
October **6** Tuesday	
October **7** Wednesday	
October **8** Thursday	
October **9** Friday	
October **10** Saturday	
October **11** Sunday	

October 12 - 18, 2020   Week 42

October **12** Monday	
October **13** Tuesday	
October **14** Wednesday	
October **15** Thursday	
October **16** Friday	
October **17** Saturday	
October **18** Sunday	

October 19 - 25, 2020   Week 43

October **19** Monday	
October **20** Tuesday	
October **21** Wednesday	
October **22** Thursday	
October **23** Friday	
October **24** Saturday	
October **25** Sunday	

October 26 - November 1, 2020   Week 44

October **26** Monday	
October **27** Tuesday	
October **28** Wednesday	
October **29** Thursday	
October **30** Friday	
October **31** Saturday	
November **1** Sunday	

Thought of the Month-November

<u>Show Me Some LOVE (Self Care)</u>

In order to function and trust that you are making the best choices for yourself, self-care is a must! Most of the time, we view self-care from a surface level, to wind down, refocus, regroup, reenergise and stop or reduce the high level of intensity we generally operate on. Examples of this include holidays, socialising, exercising, healthy eating, spending time with loved ones, lounging and reading etc. These are definitely elements of self-care.

However, 'Real' Self-care starts from instilling self-boundaries and discipline, knowing when to stop and listen, and equally knowing when to keep pushing and moving forward, as well as choosing battles and having clarity on priorities.

A major part of 'real' self-care is consciousness of who and what takes up energy; who and what fills and uplifts you. Self-care is mastering inner peace and inner confidence, permitting you to operate in a calm manner in times of challenge and chaos. 'Real' self-care is a way of life and a good habit to create, not simply a tool when it all gets too much. Mindfulness, gratefulness and appreciation of each moment is self-care. Primarily, it is about doing what feels good and what allows you to have balance and alignment on a continual basis.

Before we can genuinely care, support, love and consider others; we must first be able to do these things for ourselves. Self-care is not selfish, it is self-love.

- What do you enjoy doing mentally, physically, spiritually and emotionally that will enhance your ability to self-care?
- What boundaries and self-discipline do you need to start putting in place to allow you to self-care?

NOTES: What are your thoughts?

November 2 - 8, 2020   Week 45

November **2** Monday	
November **3** Tuesday	
November **4** Wednesday	
November **5** Thursday	
November **6** Friday	
November 7 Saturday	
November **8** Sunday	

November 9 - 15, 2020   Week 46

November **9** Monday	
November **10** Tuesday	
November **11** Wednesday	
November **12** Thursday	
November **13** Friday	
November 14 Saturday	
November **15** Sunday	

Review of Goals... AGAIN

What is your Goal?	What actions are you taking to meet this goal?	What is going well?	What needs re-thinking?
	I researched the course of my interest, location and planned a routine which will allow me to study without heavily affecting my work/life balance	I am enjoying the course as it is really beneficial and I know it will support me in progressing within my career path.	The course workload is heavier than I thought and I may need to restructure my daily routine or reduce my working hours.

November 16 - 22, 2020   Week 47

November **16** Monday	
November **17** Tuesday	
November **18** Wednesday	
November **19** Thursday	
November **20** Friday	
November 21 Saturday	
November **22** Sunday	

November 23 - 29, 2020   Week 48

November **23** Monday	
November **24** Tuesday	
November **25** Wednesday	
November **26** Thursday	
November **27** Friday	
November **28** Saturday	
November **29** Sunday	

Thought of the Month-December

Celebrate YOUR Growth & Contribution

Celebration is Recognition, Recognition is Gratitude, Gratitude is Awareness, Awareness is Responsibility, Responsibility is Empowerment, Empowerment is Motivation, Motivation is Courage, Courage is Growth, Growth is Contribution

Continue and interlink with your own words of encouragement and motivation

- What have I achieved in the last 12months which needs to be celebrated?
- What new good habits have I put in place?
- Which things have I wanted to change/ improve and managed to do so?
- How many of my goals did I meet?
- What has been my biggest learning curve?
- How have I contributed to the life of others?
- When did I last feel proud of myself?
- When did I last tell somebody that I was proud of them?
- What is the quality of my relationships? Include relationships with self, money and goals.

NOTES: What are your thoughts?

Why not start outlining your goals for 2021

November 30 - December 6, 2020   Week 49

November **30** Monday	
December **1** Tuesday	
December **2** Wednesday	
December **3** Thursday	
December **4** Friday	
December 5 Saturday	
December **6** Sunday	

December 7 - 13, 2020   Week 50

December **7** Monday	
December **8** Tuesday	
December **9** Wednesday	
December **10** Thursday	
December **11** Friday	
December **12** Saturday	
December **13** Sunday	

December 14 - 20, 2020   Week 51

December
14
Monday

December
15
Tuesday

December
16
Wednesday

December
17
Thursday

December
18
Friday

December
19
Saturday

December
20
Sunday

December 21 - 27, 2020   Week 52

December **21** Monday	
December **22** Tuesday	
December **23** Wednesday	
December **24** Thursday	
December **25** Friday	**Christmas Day**
December **26** Saturday	**Boxing Day**
December **27** Sunday	

December 28, 2020 - January 3, 2021   Week 53

December **28** Monday	Substitute day (for Boxing Day)
December **29** Tuesday	
December **30** Wednesday	
December **31** Thursday	
January **1** Friday	New Year's Day
January **2** Saturday	
January **3** Sunday	

Printed in the United States
By Bookmasters